The Songs of Flowering Trees

GOWRI CHANDRAN

BookLeaf
Publishing

Presentation by *BookLeaf Publishing*

Web: www.bookleafpub.com

E-mail: info@bookleafpub.com

ISBN: 9789357741231

First edition 2023

For my parents

Starfruit Pickles

The calloused hands of the starfruit tree
lovingly offer their fruit, tart
with life, a little sweet
with the rains of the southwest monsoon
and the leaf filtered
sunlight of the Ghats,

to my grandmother.

She cuts them into pieces of
celestial geometry, yellow green
and rubs the crevices
of the fruit with a salve of
coconut oil, salt, and flames
of red chilly.

When I mix a spoonful
of the pickles, carefully
stored in untainted bottles
with soothing cold curd and
comforting red rice,

The notes of a forgotten childhood
sing themselves back to memory.

Waterlily

On a sky dusted
liberally
with silver, untouched
by ripple or wave,
a luminous waterlily
floats, untethered,

Giving to the night
its golden pollen light.

Edible Monsoon

The trees bite off a piece
of the monsoon.

Each stormcloud baked
drop tastes
of the Emerald Dreams
of rice fields,
of the Arabian Sea's
steel grey mysteries,
and of soil,
drenched
with the potential of life

and
the leaves wear the sheen of
hunger,
satisfied.

The Geography of Germination

Across a ravine that
divides a
cotyledon continent,
a green river, tender
with youth, snakes
through,

like a spring
it bursts through
the eroded edges
of the cotyledon shelves

with the
Glorious Timidity
of new life.

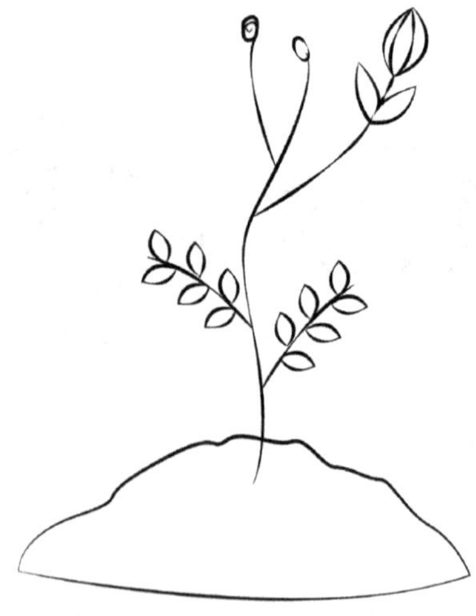

Ancestral Home

My Childhood is an ancestral home,
clinging on to memory,
desperately,
its past grandeur
a ghost
that only haunts itself,
Enter, and you'll see
a long axed mango tree, as you
breathe in the air
untainted by the city,
Listen politely
to the sparrows' stories and
drink in my old
orange candy dreams,
a little too sweet, now
buried.

The Songs of Flowering Trees

Spring delivers an
address of colour
eloquently; She
forces her audience to
listen to the
Songs of the Flowering Trees,
each verse,
a profusion of petals,
each musical note that
departs
the mouth of the tree,
a gift
wrapped in the
festivity of young life,
deposited
at the doorways
of city- stained hearts
by a heady, intoxicating breeze.

February Mornings

On February mornings, warm
enough to drink, warm
enough to douse
winter's icy flames,
There is something sweeter
and more concrete in
the melodies
of the songbirds

On February mornings, warm
enough to carry in pockets
like hot potatoes
I run my fingers
through birdsong
and drape it around my
neck like a scarf
of silk.

Dear leaf

It is time,
dear leaf
to wash off the cold
that clings
to your veins,
It is time
for your
rain parched topography
to relearn
Life again;
A hundred different greens
wait
by your doors, to call
you home,
dear leaf,
Spring is almost here,
Shed your winter
toughness,
be soft,
It is time.

Fruits for a Waxing Moon

On boughs
of sky tinted
vermillion
by the setting sun,
purple splotches
of night-
ripe fruit
for the moon
to bite into;
sweet enough to
numb
her growing pains.

Boiled Groundnuts

Within a newspaper spout
boiled groundnuts

punctuated by
fragments of onion
exclamations of coriander
and the spice of the Bay of Bengal,

each little pearl, a song
of the earth, a flicker
of hope that glimmers
in the seller's eyes as she
ladles out her wares
with a gratitude laden smile,

warmer
than boiled groundnuts
within a newspaper spout.

Magic

Magic
in the rainbows that live
on the necks of pigeons,
in rough lines inscribed like
language onto trees,
in the architecture
of flower petals,
and in a leaf saturated breeze,
Magic
in words fed on
kindness and love, and
in the sepia sweetness
of memory
Magic
in the comforting chaos
of city streets
and in being lost in a
flowery, Spring day dream.

Tides

The moon howls.

It sings
a wolf song, written
only for the sea
to hear
and when the sea
adsorbs every
verse of
cold silver
crater and
hunger
she dances
Spring and Neap Tides.

Branches like roots

Into the lush earth
of a sky, fractured
by green,
an oak
sinks in its branches,
hungry
like the roots that
snake through water
untouched land
longingly
resentfully
mournfully mirroring
river tributaries.

Summer

Summer writes
rose apples that
bloom like blushes
on love touched trees
on flower petal paper,
delicate
Summer leaves
splotches of bone dry brown,
From leaf laden branches
Summer coaxes
out a festival of flower,
an outpouring
of colour,
and on an expanse of sky,
a poem of clearest blue,
Summer writes.

Forest fires

One day, we became forest fires.

We singed away
every imprint of
the colour green,
We made ashes
of life under soot
stained skies,
the trees crumbled
beneath our feet

like hope, in war, and
as the monsoon began
losing its way,
Peace became a memory.

One day, we became forest fires
and we burned each other.

Cobweb

I am more cobweb
than human these days,
I am silken threads
of architectural splendor,
draped
across splintered wood
in houses
haunted by memory,
vulnerably and
threateningly alive, I am
filaments made of Moon
that threaten to
come apart,
I dissipate
like incense smoke
in large rooms

when disturbed.

Of Sadness

Sadness
Labyrinthine
corn maze
stretching across
a few continents,
dark clouds
leering above
bloody lands
dark
clouds that do not
carry any of
Monsoon's mercy,
Sadness, easy
to get used to,
Sadness slipping
in and coating
the walls of
any place that looks
like Home
with mildew, until one
forgets what the
walls looked like before

Sadness.

Dusk

I turn into dusk,
Sometimes

I force the sun into slumber,
Every fragment
of birdsong
deserts me;
the parrots with
their voices of summer,
leave, like mist does on
Mornings of molten gold
every tint of noisy colour
becomes a

declaration of transience,
a verse of apology,
a Eulogy in and of itself.

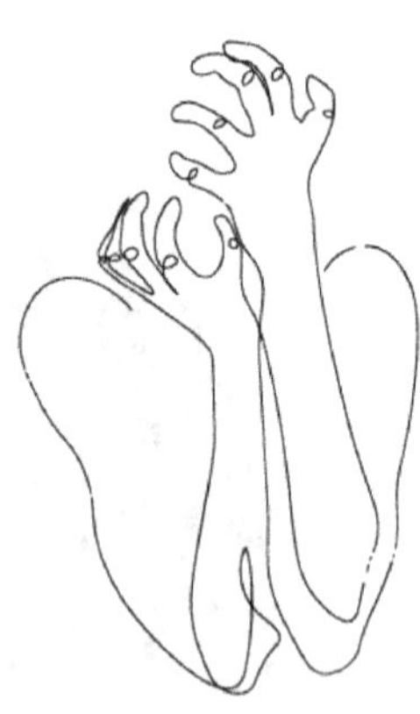

Languages

I do not speak People fluently

I forget faces and names like
people are small tea shops that dot
national highways,
People is
a language I stutter through,
but
there are languages I speak
as well as my heart speaks rhythm;
I can write books in the
Tenderness of Spring, I can
codify the grammar of the
Death of Flowers and the Tyranny of Sweet fruit,
I can deliver lectures in the
Rust of history,

There are languages that the trees
taught me, some languages, I
lisp through with clarity, and
Sadness,

Sadness is a language I taught
myself and I find that it's
sickly sweet dialect taints the cadences
of all the other languages I speak.

Metaphors that are kind

Today, my metaphors will be kind.
The cities that
populate my poetry
will bloom like vines of
honeysuckle growing
on windowsills,
Wrinkles on hands
will be river tributaries
overflowing with stories;
Old age, a process of geomorphology
Absence will be a
resting home for a love
that lingers, like the many
ghosts of the sun, at dusk
and adulthood will be
a treasure hunt; it will be the
sweet trial of prising open a
jackfruit, to find
ingots of molten honey.

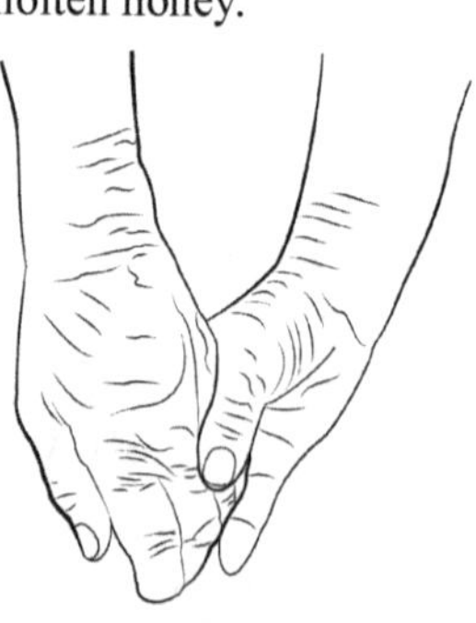

Disjointed Haikus

Leaves, lattice windows
that throw to the earth, light shards;
crowns of old fort trees.
~Jaali

Golden wagging tails
in the hearts of wind swept ferns
Joy speaks the same way.
~Shared vocabulary

Fingerprints of Spring
in soft thunderclouds that bloom
The flowers live on
~Memories

From blood vibrant earth
A declaration of life
Seedlings after rain
~Birth

The seasons, sigh-short
seperate- beautifully
disjointed Haikus

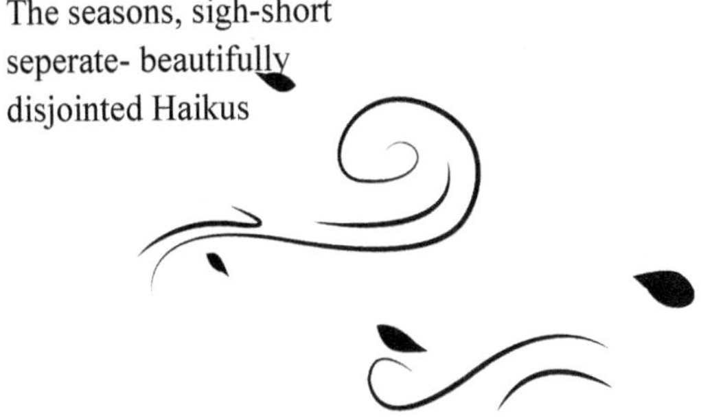